ST. KITTS AND NEVIS TRAVEL

GUIDE 2023 - 2024

St. Kitts and Nevis Uncovered: Your
Ultimate Guide for Exploring the Twin
Treasures of the Caribbean - From Pristine
Beaches to Historical Wonders

Sarah T. Burton

ALL RIGHTS RESERVED.

No part of this publication may be reproduced,distributed or transmitted in any form or by any means including photocopying, recording or other electronic or mechanical methods without the prior written permission of the publisher, except in the case of brief quotations embedded in critical reviews and certain other noncommercial uses permitted by copyright law.

Copyright © Sarah T. Burton, 2023

Table Of Content

My Memorable Vacation Experiences

A unique experience can be had by traveling to St. Kitts and Nevis, where the blend of natural beauty, rich history, and friendly culture offers an enchanting voyage into the heart of the Caribbean. My trip to these twin islands left a lasting impression as I took in the breathtaking scenery, discovered historical artifacts, and forged relationships with the hospitable locals.

The expedition started with the arrival at St. Kitts' Robert L. Bradshaw International Airport, where the sight of Mount Liamuiga rising in the distance foreshadowed the exploits to come. The first few days were spent in St. Kitts, the bigger of the two islands, which we explored. The geography of the island was diversified, providing a variety of activities.

The ascent of Mount Liamuiga, the dormant volcano that towers over St. Kitts, was among the highlights.

Although difficult, the ascent was a worthwhile experience. We came across fascinating flora and fauna as we winded through lush rainforests, from colorful flowers to amusing green vervet monkeys. The panoramic views of the island and the surrounding Caribbean Sea were truly stunning as we ascended to the summit. It was a triumphant and humbling experience that made me appreciate how these islands are shaped by extraordinary natural forces.

St. Kitts' history side was quite fascinating. A UNESCO World Heritage Site and masterpiece of colonial military construction, Brimstone Hill Fortress National Park, was one of the places we visited. The enormous stone walls, built on a volcanic hill, provided a window into the turbulent past of the island. I nearly felt like I could hear the echoes of history and the strategic importance of this fort during colonial times as I walked through the beautifully preserved barracks and guns.

We took a detour to Frigate Bay, a gorgeous beach with soft sand and enticing blue waters, for a change of scenery. Here, leisurely activities like lounging beneath swaying palm trees and swimming in the warm Caribbean Sea were the order of the day. Ample options for snorkeling, paddleboarding, and even catamaran tours to explore the coastline were available for water activity lovers.

We took the short ferry ride to Nevis to continue our journey. Nevis had a certain charm because of its smaller size and slower tempo. Nevis Peak, the highest point on the island, beckoned us to start another strenuous walk. The breathtaking views of Nevis and the nearby islands were the reward for the hike. We came upon abandoned sugar mills and plantation homes along the road, artifacts from a bygone period that added to the island's history.

Charlestown, the nation's capital, was a trip back in time. The town's cobbled streets and maintained Georgian architecture emanated a colonial charm. We went to the Alexander Hamilton Museum, which is located in the house where the first Secretary of the Treasury of the

United States was born. His Nevisian ancestry was a fascinating historical side trip, I discovered.

The warmth of the people of St. Kitts and Nevis will never be forgotten. We felt welcomed by the Caribbean atmosphere, from the kind smiles of the residents to the energetic music and dance during cultural events. With meals like "Stewed Saltfish and Johnny Cake" and freshly caught shellfish seasoned with a symphony of spices, we indulged in the local cuisine.

1. Introduction

1.1 Overview Of St. Kitts and Nevis

The fascinating two-island nation of St. Kitts and Nevis is situated in the Caribbean Sea and is formally referred to as the Federation of Saint Christopher and Nevis. This magnificent archipelago, which is located in the Leeward Islands of the West Indies, is well-known for its outstanding natural beauty, extensive history, and dynamic culture.

Geographically speaking, St. Kitts and Nevis is the Western Hemisphere's smallest sovereign state in terms of both land and population. The bigger of the two islands, Saint Kitts, is frequently referred to as "The Mother Colony of the West Indies" because of its historical importance during the colonial era. Nevis, its younger twin, is a favored vacation spot for tourists looking to unwind because of its more relaxed and serene ambiance.

The strands of colonialism, the fight for independence, and cultural diversity are woven together in the history of St. Kitts and Nevis to create a tapestry. During the 17th and 18th centuries, European nations, especially the British and the French, competed for the sovereignty of these islands. The architecture, customs and even some towns' and landmarks' names still bear traces of this colonial past.

Brimstone Hill Fortress National Park, a UNESCO World Heritage Site, is one of St. Kitts' most well-known historical locations. Built by the British in the 17th century to stave against prospective invasions, this strong castle is a testimony to the era's architectural prowess. Visitors can stroll around its ramparts, which have been restored, and take in expansive views of the surroundings.

St. Kitts and Nevis's culture is a colorful tapestry that reflects the blending of African, European, and native Caribbean influences. Calypso and reggae music are frequently used to set the pace of life here, and the people are renowned for their kind hospitality. Festivals and festivities, like Carnival, are an important component of the cultural landscape and give visitors a sense of the vivacious energy of the islands.

St. Kitts and Nevis has a delicious blend of flavors in its cuisine. A common ingredient is seafood, and local favorites include conch chowder and spiny lobster. The islands are especially well-known for their succulent, wonderfully sweet, and sweet mangoes, which are frequently eaten either fresh or as a component of regional recipes.

On these islands, nature lovers will find a wealth of things to discover. Green vervet monkeys and a large number of other bird species can be found in the lush jungles of St. Kitts. Nevis provides trekking opportunities to discover the island's untamed beauty because of its volcanic landscape.

Luxury resorts and immaculate beaches have helped St. Kitts and Nevis become more well-known as a location for luxury travel in recent years, drawing tourists from all over the world. By drawing in investors looking for second citizenship, the Citizenship by Investment Program has also aided in economic expansion.

1.2 Culture and History

St. Kitts and Nevis's history and culture are intricately entwined, reflecting centuries of colonial influence and a thriving Caribbean tradition. Let's explore this island's intriguing history.

The Kalinago, the native inhabitants of St. Kitts and Nevis, first lived there. The islands were first discovered by Europeans in 1493, when Christopher Columbus, on his second voyage to the Americas, touched down on St. Kitts. The culture and customs of the islands were drastically altered by later European colonization, especially those carried out by the British and French.

When sugar production became the primary industry, enslaved Africans were imported to labor on sugar plantations. The islands still honor their African heritage through music, dance, and traditional customs today since this sad chapter in history left a lasting effect on them.

Brimstone Hill Fortress National Park is one of St. Kitts and Nevis' most important historical landmarks. This UNESCO World Heritage Site is proof of the strategic value of the islands throughout the colonial era. The stronghold, which is positioned atop a commanding hill, provides panoramic views of the surrounding area and provides insight into the military architecture of the 17th and 18th centuries.

In 1983, the British colonial power over the islands was ended, and they became the Federation of Saint Kitts and Nevis. They have since accepted their newfound independence while conserving their extensive cultural history.

In St. Kitts and Nevis, music and dancing are an essential element of daily life. During boisterous festivals and festivities, calypso and reggae rhythms permeate the air, and traditional dances like the masquerade and the bull are enthusiastically performed.

African, European, and Caribbean elements are blended in St. Kitts and Nevis cuisine. They frequently prepare fish, conch, and other seafood with fragrant spices and serve it with side dishes like rice and peas as a mainstay of their diet. The national cuisine of the islands, "Stewed Saltfish and Johnny Cake," is delectable and a must-try.

1.3 Climate and Geography

St. Kitts and Nevis' topography and climate play a crucial role in molding both the natural beauty and way of life of the islands, adding to their allure. The unique topography and tropical temperature of these two Caribbean gems, which are part of the Lesser Antilles, make them a year-round tourist haven.

Geographically, St. Kitts and Nevis are a part of the Eastern Caribbean's volcanic island arc. The bigger of the two islands, St. Kitts, is distinguished by Mount Liamuiga, a towering 3,792 feet (1,156 meters) volcanic peak in the center. Despite being dormant, the volcano continues to contribute to the island's rich, fertile soil, which is ideal for agriculture. The majority of the interior is covered in rolling hills and lush rainforests, while the mountains are surrounded by a fertile coastal plain.

In contrast, Nevis is frequently referred to as the "Queen of the Caribees" due to its delicate, conical shape. Nevis Peak, an additional extinct volcano that rises to a height of 3,232 feet (985 meters), dominates the area. Nevis is renowned for its lush greenery, serene atmosphere, and fertile, green scenery.

A narrow canal known as "The Narrows," which is only two miles wide at its narrowest point, divides the islands. Due to their close vicinity, visitors may easily spend time exploring both islands and taking in their charms.

Let's now discuss the weather. Due to their location in the Caribbean Sea, St. Kitts and Nevis have a tropical climate. This entails mild weather and steady trade breezes all year round. Tourists can enjoy a cozy and welcoming environment thanks to the average temperature, which ranges from 79 to 88 degrees Fahrenheit (26 to 31 degrees Celsius).

The dry season, which normally lasts from December to April, and the wet season, which lasts from May to November, are the two main seasons on the islands. Although there are greater downpours during the rainy season, they are typically followed by sunny skies and brief afternoon showers. Travelers should keep an eye on weather forecasts if planning a trip during these months as it also happens to be hurricane season in the Caribbean at this time of year.

The trade winds are essential for regulating the climate and keeping temperatures comfortable. They also make St. Kitts and Nevis a well-liked vacation spot for sailors and fans of other water sports. The waters around the islands are crystal clear and turquoise, making them perfect for water sports like windsurfing.

Both islands' excellent soil and abundant vegetation are a direct result of their volcanic origins and regular rains. The rich flora, which covers the area with a variety of tropical plants, fruit trees, and vivid flowers, demonstrates this natural bounty.

1.4 Quick Facts About St. Kitts and Nevis

A few short facts about St. Kitts and Nevis are as follows:

1. Federation of Saint Kitts and Nevis is its official name.

2. Location: The Lesser Antilles' Eastern Caribbean region includes the two islands that makeup St. Kitts and Nevis.

3. Size: Nevis is roughly 36 square miles (93 square kilometers) in size, while St. Kitts is roughly 68 square miles (176 square kilometers).

4. Basseterre, a city on the island of St. Kitts, serves as the nation's capital.

5. As of 2021, it was predicted that St. Kitts and Nevis had a population of about 53,000.

6. The official language of the islands is English.

7. Although the United States Dollar (USD) is widely accepted, the Eastern Caribbean Dollar (XCD) is the official unit of currency.

8. Government: The British monarch is the head of state in St. Kitts and Nevis, which is a parliamentary democracy with a constitutional monarchy.

9. On September 19, 1983, the islands declared their independence from British colonial authority.

10. Economy: The nation's economy is largely supported by offshore banking, agriculture, and tourism.

11. Famous Landmarks: Among the prominent landmarks are the picturesque Nevis Peak and the Brimstone Hill Fortress National Park, both of which are included as UNESCO World Heritage Sites.

12. A tropical marine climate characterizes the islands, with the dry season lasting from December to April and the rainy season lasting from May to November.

13. St. Kitts and Nevis experience a hurricane season from June to November.

14. Standard Time in the Atlantic (AST)

15. Driving is done on the left side of the road.

16. Electricity: 230V/60Hz (plugs in North American configuration)

17. Robert L. Bradshaw International Airport (St. Kitts) is a significant airport.

18. National Symbols: The national flag has two white stars to signify St. Kitts and Nevis, together with the colors green for Nevis, yellow for the sun, and red for the fight for freedom.

19. "Country Above Self" is the country's motto.

20. Emergency Contacts: 1233
- 911 for the police
- 911 - Ambulance
- 911 for the fire department

These fast facts give a brief overview of St. Kitts and Nevis, but there is still a lot to learn about these alluring Caribbean islands.

2. Important Preparation For Your Travel

2.1 Travel Documents and Visa Requirements

Many people have a desire to visit St. Kitts and Nevis, the charming twin islands in the Caribbean. Understanding visa regulations and relevant travel documentation is crucial for ensuring a smooth and hassle-free vacation. Here is a detailed guide to the travel documents you'll need, regardless of whether you're organizing a quick getaway or a lengthy stay.

Visa Prerequisites:

In comparison to some other destinations, St. Kitts and Nevis has comparatively lax visa requirements. However, depending on your country and the reason for your visit, the particular requirements may change. Here are some important things to think about:

1. Visa-Free Travel: For stays up to 90 days, nationals of several nations—including the United States, Canada, the United Kingdom, and the majority of European Union countries—do not need a visa. These nationals do not require a visa to visit relatives, do business, or engage in tourism in St. Kitts and Nevis.

2. Validity of Passport: Ensure that your passport is valid for at least six months after the day you want to leave St. Kitts and Nevis. This is a widespread requirement that is strictly upheld in many nations.

3. Return Ticket: To ensure that you do not intend to stay longer than is permitted, immigration authorities may ask for documentation of a return or onward ticket.

4. Visa for Longer Stays: You'll probably need to apply for a particular visa if you plan to stay in St. Kitts and Nevis for more than 90 days for reasons like job, study, or habitation. Your specific situation will determine the sort of visa needed, so it's best to contact the St. Kitts

and Nevis embassy or consulate in your area for further information.

5. Visa Extension: The Immigration Department will help you if you already reside in St. Kitts and Nevis and need to prolong your stay. However, extensions are frequently given for particular circumstances, such as medical care or personal crises.

6. Immunization Requirements: St. Kitts and Nevis does not have any particular immunization requirements for visitors as of my most recent information update in September 2021. However, given the rapidly changing nature of the global health situation, it is imperative to remain informed about any changes or medically related requirements.

Travel documents include:
When traveling to St. Kitts and Nevis, you should have the following paperwork and belongings in order in addition to your passport and visa:

1. Travel insurance is strongly advised, however, it is not required. It can offer protection against unforeseen situations like trip cancellations and medical issues.

2. Carry a copy of the reservation confirmation for your hotel or other lodging, as immigration authorities may ask for it.

3. Currency: Bring enough money to cover your stay in St. Kitts and Nevis in a form that is accepted there (often US dollars or Eastern Caribbean dollars).

4. Vacation Itinerary: It's a good idea to have a copy of your vacation itinerary, which should include information about your flights and the things you intend to do.

5. Keep a list of crucial phone numbers handy, including those for the local emergency services and the embassy or consulate of your nation in St. Kitts and Nevis.

2.2 The Ideal Time to Travel

The ideal time to visit the alluring Caribbean islands of St. Kitts and Nevis will largely depend on your interests and what you intend to get out of your trip. Although the islands have good weather year-round, certain seasons are better suited to particular pursuits.

1. From December to April, the high season
The dry season coincides with the high season in St. Kitts and Nevis, making this the busiest travel period. What to anticipate throughout this time is as follows:

- Ideal Weather: The islands have their driest and coziest weather from December to April. The weather will be beautiful, with lots of sunlight, clear skies, and highs of about 81°F (27°C).

- Exciting Festivals: This is a terrific time to travel if you're interested in taking in the local culture and celebrations. Numerous occasions, such as regattas, music festivals, and Carnival celebrations, are held on St. Kitts and Nevis.

- Water Sports: This season is ideal for snorkeling, diving, and other water sports due to the calm seas and excellent underwater visibility.

- Peak Travel Season: Keep in mind that this is the busiest time for travel, so expect higher hotel and flight prices as well as possible crowds at famous destinations during this period. Booking far in advance is advisable.

2. May to June, the shoulder season

Between the wet season and high season, St. Kitts and Nevis experiences the shoulder season. The weather is still beautiful, and rates are reasonable.

- Less Crowds: Compared to the high season, May and June see fewer visitors, allowing you to explore the islands in peace.

- Lower Prices: This is a good time to travel if you're looking for a good deal because hotels and flights tend to be more affordable.

- Occasional Showers: As the islands enter the rainy season, there may be sporadic showers of rain despite the otherwise beautiful weather.

3. From July through November, it rains
Hurricane season in the Caribbean coincides with the rainy season in St. Kitts and Nevis. What to think about in this time frame is as follows:

- Lush Greenery: The rain brings lush, bright flora to the islands, providing nature lovers and photographers with an exquisite backdrop.

- Fewer People: Since tourism declines during the rainy season, you'll be able to take advantage of a calmer, more laid-back atmosphere.

- Hurricane Risk: Be mindful of the likelihood of hurricanes, particularly in September and October. Even while most storms won't damage modern infrastructure, it's still important to keep aware and be ready.

- Water Activities: Even if sporadic downpours are to be expected, you can still engage in water sports. Short bouts of rain are usually followed by sunny intervals.

The ideal time to travel to St. Kitts and Nevis ultimately depends on your priorities.

2.3 Exchange Rates and Money

When organizing a vacation to St. Kitts and Nevis, it is essential to comprehend the local currency and conversion rates. Although the United States Dollar (USD) is commonly accepted, these islands utilize the Eastern Caribbean Dollar (XCD) as their official currency. Here is a thorough manual to assist you in handling your money while you are here.

A. Currency:

1. The official currency of St. Kitts and Nevis, as well as several other Caribbean countries that belong to the Eastern Caribbean Currency Union, is the Eastern Caribbean Dollar (XCD). Banknotes and coins come in a variety of denominations, including 5, 10, 20, 50, and 100 XCD notes as well as cent coins. It is abbreviated as XCD and is sometimes symbolized by the symbol "$" or "EC$."

2. Dollar of the United States (USD): The Eastern Caribbean Dollar and the Dollar of the United States are both commonly accepted and used in St. Kitts and Nevis. International travelers will find it helpful that many shops, lodgings, and restaurants list pricing in both XCD and USD.

B. Rates of Exchange

It is essential to research the most recent exchange rates before your travel because the value of the Eastern Caribbean Dollar is subject to fluctuation. Both the Vance W. Amory International Airport in Nevis and the

Robert L. Bradshaw International Airport in St. Kitts offer exchange services. Additionally, there are local banks and exchange offices all around the islands where you can exchange money.

C. Using ATMs and credit cards

In St. Kitts and Nevis, credit cards, including Visa and MasterCard, are commonly accepted, particularly at bigger venues like hotels and restaurants. For smaller shops and marketplaces, it's a good idea to have some cash on hand.

Both islands have ATMs, allowing for easy access to money. The majority of ATMs accept the most popular international debit and credit cards, but it's a good idea to let your bank know about your travel itinerary to avoid any problems using your card when traveling overseas.

D. Checks for Travel:

Traveler's checks used to be a popular method of carrying money while traveling, but their use has decreased recently. Traveler's checks aren't widely accepted in St. Kitts and Nevis, so it's more practical to use credit cards and cash instead.

E. Money Exchange Advice:

1. When you arrive at the airport, exchange some money or get Eastern Caribbean Dollars from an ATM to cover immediate needs.

2. To get the most for your money, compare conversion rates at banks and exchange bureaus.

3. For daily expenses including tipping, keep modest currencies on hand.

4. To avoid getting overcharged or undercharged, become familiar with the current exchange rate.

2.4 Communication and Language

In every vacation experience, communication and language are crucial, and English is the official language of St. Kitts and Nevis. However, local accents and communication methods have also been influenced by the culture and history of the islands, giving interpersonal interactions more nuance.

1. Official Language: St. Kitts and Nevis's official language is English. As a result, English is used in official settings such as those in government, education, and business. You won't have any issue speaking English as a traveler the entire way.

2. Local dialects: Although English is the preferred language, you might hear various variations of it. "Kittitian" or "Nevisian Creole," regional dialects influenced by African, French, and West Indian languages, are two examples. The local population and informal settings are where these dialects are most commonly heard. You can come across unusual sayings and idioms while visiting that are a reflection of the island's rich cultural heritage.

3. The inhabitants of St. Kitts and Nevis are renowned for their polite and cordial communication style. When

meeting someone for the first time, it's polite to extend a greeting. In addition to a handshake and a smile, greeting someone with a courtesy title like "Mr." or "Mrs." is considered respectful.

4. Communication and tourism: Due to the islands' emphasis on tourism, many locals are used to communicating with visitors. You'll discover that the majority of service providers, including hotel staff, tour guides, and restaurant staff, are fluent in English and able to help tourists.

5. Local Phrases and Expressions: Even though English is the primary language, it might be entertaining to acquire a few regional expressions and phrases to better understand the local way of life. For instance, "lime" denotes a place to hang out or unwind, "ting" designates an item, and "massa" is a casual way to address someone. While not compulsory for communicating, employing these expressions can improve your interactions and experience.

6. Cultural Sensitivity: When engaging with natives in any destination, it's crucial to be respectful of their culture and attentive to their needs. When you visit, being courteous and polite will go a long way toward fostering goodwill.

7. Technology and Connectivity: St. Kitts and Nevis has a cutting-edge communications network, providing access to the internet and mobile networks. The majority of hotels and eateries include Wi-Fi, enabling you to remain in touch with loved ones or plan your route using smartphone apps and maps.

2.5 Essentials for Traveling

It's important to strike a balance between practicality and casual comfort while packing for a trip to the beautiful Caribbean islands of St. Kitts and Nevis. The tropical weather and variety of activities on the islands necessitate cautious packing. The following list of necessities will help you have a comfortable and pleasurable stay.

1. Pack breathable, lightweight clothing because St. Kitts and Nevis have a tropical environment. Fabrics made of cotton and linen are excellent for keeping you cool and cozy. For trips to the beach, don't forget your swimsuits, and think about bringing a cover-up for sun protection.

2. Sun protection: To protect oneself from the Caribbean sun, you should wear sunscreen, sunglasses, and a wide-brimmed hat. Be ready since the sun can be very strong, especially in the dry season.

3. Repellent for insects: Although seldom a serious problem, insects, particularly mosquitoes, can be found, especially in lush places. To keep comfortable while engaging in outside activities, bring bug repellent.

4. Comfortable Footwear: If you intend to trek the volcanoes or explore the islands' nature trails, you must wear comfortable walking shoes or sandals with adequate traction. Flip-flops and other beach shoes are appropriate for relaxing beach days.

5. Pack a lightweight rain jacket or umbrella if you're traveling during the rainy season (June to November) so you can stay dry during brief downpours.

6. Travel adapters are necessary if your gadgets have various plug types because St. Kitts and Nevis use Type A and Type B electrical outlets.

7. Travel documents: Make sure you have your passport, any necessary visas, tickets for your flights, and hotel reservations. Carrying photocopies or digital copies of these documents is a smart idea.

8. Prescription drugs should be brought with an adequate supply, along with a copy of your prescription, if you have them. Think about bringing a first-aid kit that includes supplies like sticky bandages, antiseptic wipes, and painkillers.

9. Despite not being a tangible object, having travel insurance is crucial. It can offer protection against

unanticipated events like trip cancellations and medical issues.

10. Water bottle: It's important to stay hydrated in the Caribbean heat. Bring a reusable water bottle that you can fill up all day.

11. Beach accessories: Pack items like a beach towel, beach bag, and snorkeling equipment if you have it if you intend to spend time on the stunning beaches.

12. Electronics and cameras: Use a camera or smartphone to capture the stunning scenery of the islands. Don't forget to pack extra memory cards and chargers.

13. Even though the environment on the islands is laid-back, if you want to go out to fine restaurants or enjoy the nightlife, you may want to pack some casual evening wear.

14. Cash and Credit Cards: Although credit cards are extensively used, it's a good idea to have some cash on hand in USD or ECD for small purchases and locations that might not accept cards.

15. Adapter for Driving: If you intend to drive in St. Kitts and Nevis when renting a car, don't forget to include an adapter for left-handed driving.

16. Snorkeling equipment: If you enjoy snorkeling, think about bringing your mask, snorkel, and fins on your trip to explore the fascinating underwater world.

17. Travel locks: Use travel locks on your suitcases to keep your belongings safe.

18. When you're on the go and need to keep your electronics charged, a portable power bank can be a lifesaver.

19. Physical maps and guidebooks can be useful for exploring without relying on internet connectivity, even though digital navigation is more convenient.

20. Last but not least, bring a sense of patience and an open mind. Positivity can improve your trip because unexpected occurrences are a common part of exploring new areas.

Consider adjusting your packing list to reflect your unique interests and hobbies. Your trip to St. Kitts and Nevis will be one to remember whether you spend it exploring the lush rainforests, relaxing on stunning beaches, or taking in the local culture.

3. Gastronomic Treats And Beverages

3.1 Regional Foods & Dishes

Discovering the St. Kitts and Nevis culinary offerings is a delightful voyage into Caribbean cuisine laced with regional flavors and outside influences. These islands provide a wide variety of delicacies that highlight their rich natural resources, history, and culture. Here's a detailed look at some of the must-try local dishes and cuisine.

1. The traditional Kittitian cuisine saltfish and bakes are made with salt cod that has been simmered in milk and spices before being mashed and baked in dough. It frequently comes with a side of sweet potatoes or fried plantains.

2. Using rice, chicken, sausage, shrimp, crab, and vegetables, jambalaya is a Creole cuisine. It frequently comes with a side of crackers or bread.

3. Flying fish is a popular grilled or fried local fish. It frequently comes with a side of veggies or rice and peas.

4. Ackee and Saltfish is a Jamaican meal made with salt cod and the fruit ackee, which is indigenous to West Africa. It frequently comes with a side of bread or fried plantains.

5. Stew made with meat, vegetables, and spices is known as a pepperpot. It frequently comes with rice or bread on the side.

6. Don't let the name of this meal mislead you; there isn't any actual goat meat in it. Goat (or occasionally cattle) meat, breadfruit, and a variety of spices are combined to make the hearty stew known as "Goat Water." It's a soul-warming comfort cuisine that honors the culinary history of the islands.

7. Roti: A favorite dish in St. Kitts and Nevis, Roti is influenced by the East Indian community. It consists of a flatbread stuffed with different foods, like curried goat, chicken, or veggies. It is a flavorful and satisfying supper because of the combination of flavors and spices.

8. Callaloo Soup: Made from a leafy green that resembles spinach, callaloo, this substantial soup is frequently served as a side dish. It is frequently made with coconut milk and spiced, giving it a creamy and mildly spicy flavor.

9. Rice, pigeon peas, chicken or beef, and herbs and spices are all cooked together in a single pot to create the cuisine known as "pelau." The result is a delicious and satisfying dish that is popular at gatherings and special occasions.

10. Breadfruit is a staple in the Caribbean and can be cooked in several ways, including as frying, boiling, or roasting. A popular side dish with a distinct texture and flavor is fried breadfruit.

11. Rum Punch: Trying the native rum is a must when visiting the Caribbean. Rum is produced in St. Kitts and Nevis, where "Rum Punch" is a popular beverage. Typically, rum, fruit juices, and spices are combined to make this delicious and strong beverage.

12. Learn about the several local fruits, including mangoes, papayas, guavas, and passion fruit, that are cultivated on the islands. They are frequently consumed either raw or in fruit salads.

13. Street Food: Make sure to try some of the "Jerk Chicken" that local food vendors are selling as street food. These meals highlight the vivid tastes of the islands and are a great way to sample real Caribbean food.

Additionally, St. Kitts and Nevis has a wide variety of delectable treats, including:

1. Guava, sugar, and spices are used to make the classic Kittitian dish known as "guava cheese." It frequently comes with ice cream or whipped cream on the side.

2. Coconut Drops: Coconut, sugar, and spices are combined to make these tiny, fried desserts. They frequently come with a cup of coffee or tea on the side.

3. Soft, fried doughnuts called "jelly doughnuts" are frequently filled with jelly or custard. They frequently come with a side of syrup or powdered sugar.

3.2 Dining Protocol and Practices

Dining in St. Kitts and Nevis is a cultural experience that showcases the warmth, friendliness, and rich history of the islands. Your eating experiences can be improved and you can guarantee that you respect the local culture by being aware of the dining etiquette and customs. Here is a detailed explanation of St. Kitts and Nevis's dining traditions:

1. Respectful Greetings: It is usual to extend a courteous greeting before visiting a restaurant or someone's house. It's customary to address someone with polite titles like "Mr." or "Mrs." and handshakes are appreciated.

2. Despite the laid-back ambiance on the islands, certain expensive restaurants may impose dress rules. It's a good idea to find out in advance whether there are any dress codes for a particular venue.

3. Punctuality: It is nice to arrive on time for dinner invites or reservations. Respect for the hosts' time and effort is demonstrated by showing up a little early or on time.

4. Tipping is expected and appreciated by service providers in St. Kitts and Nevis. Restaurant invoices typically include a 10-15% gratuity, but it's best practice to verify the bill and leave a bigger tip if you like.

5. Dining Etiquette: Chinese table manners are comparable to Western traditions. Wait until everyone has been served before beginning your meal, use utensils

from the outside in, and refrain from using your elbows on the table.

6. Local customs: Express your admiration for the regional food by sampling delicacies like Saltfish and Johnny Cake or goat water. It's a great chance to discover the culinary history of the islands.

7. Island Music: Live music is a common component in many dining establishments, frequently adding Caribbean rhythms. Accept the lively music and feel free to join in the dancing if the mood hits.

8. Food Preferences: It's a good idea to let your server know in advance if you have any food preferences or allergies. The majority of places are accommodative and can provide several menu selections.

9. Giving Thanks: It's traditional to give your hosts or the restaurant staff a "Thank you" or a "Thanks for the meal" after a meal to show your appreciation.

10. If you have leftover food from a meal, you may request a "doggie bag" from the restaurant. However, it's courteous to consume your entire meal when visiting someone's home.

3.3 Local Food Markets and Cooking Classes

In St. Kitts and Nevis, shopping at neighborhood markets and taking cooking classes are rewarding experiences that let you fully appreciate the local cuisine. These activities offer a special chance to find out about local foods, learn about conventional culinary methods, and interact with the neighborhood.

Local grocery stores:

1. Basseterre Public Market (St. Kitts): This lively market is a sensory joy and is situated in the center of Basseterre, the island nation's capital. Fresh fruits, vegetables, spices, and locally caught seafood are displayed in vibrant ways. It's a great spot to try

uncommon fruits like breadfruit and soursop. From Monday through Saturday, it is open.

2. Nevis Market: Located in Charlestown, this market is the biggest on Nevis. From Tuesday to Saturday, it is open.

3. Old Road Market is a more compact market that is situated in that area of St. Kitts. From Wednesday to Sunday, it is open.

4. Charlestown Market on Nevis: Charlestown is home to a quaint market. You can browse the stalls here to find everything from locally crafted crafts to fresh produce. The market is renowned for its colorful assortment of fruits and vegetables.

5. Farmers' markets: On occasion, St. Kitts and Nevis hold farmers' markets when local producers and craftspeople congregate to display their wares. These markets are excellent places to buy fruits, vegetables, handmade items, and other organic products straight from the growers.

6. In addition to food markets, you can also discover craft markets where local artisans sell their wares like pottery, colorful textiles, and woven baskets. These markets provide a window into the artistic traditions of the islands.

Cooking lessons:

1. The Fairview Great House in St. Kitts hosts the Caribbean Cooks cooking class, which teaches you how to prepare local specialties like pepperpot, jambalaya, and saltfish and bakes.

2. The Montpelier Plantation Inn in Nevis hosts the Taste of Nevis Cooking Class, which teaches you how to prepare regional specialties including conch fritters, callaloo soup, and ginger beer.

3. Learn how to make classic Caribbean drinks like the Painkiller and the Planter's Punch at the Rum Runners Bar in St. Kitts during the cooking lesson there.

4. Belle Mont Farm (St. Kitts): Learn to prepare farm-to-table meals with fresh vegetables from their organic farm by enrolling in one of their culinary programs. It is a culinary experience that combines sustainability and education.

5. Private Cooking courses: In St. Kitts and Nevis, certain eateries and chefs provide private, individualized cooking courses. You can plan a tailored dining experience, whether your preferences are seafood, curries, or regional pastries.

6. Community Cooking Workshops: Occasionally, cultural institutions and community organizations hold cooking classes that shed light on the islanders' culinary customs. These gatherings frequently include opportunities to sample regional cuisine and hands-on cooking lessons.

3.4 Options that are Vegetarian and Vegan

While seafood and meat dishes are popular in St. Kitts and Nevis, there are also fulfilling options for vegetarians and vegans. The islands' restaurants and eateries are becoming more tolerant of dietary restrictions. Here are some recommendations for restaurants that provide vegetarian and vegan food:

1. The Green Elephant in Basseterre has a wide range of curries, stir-fries, and salads that are vegetarian and vegan-friendly.

2. The Hungry Bun in Charlestown serves a variety of vegan cuisine with Caribbean influences, including jerk tofu and plantain curry.

3. The Spice Merchant in Basseterre serves a variety of vegetarian and vegan cuisine with Indian influences, including dal makhani and aloo gobi.

4. Local Markets: For a large variety of fresh fruits and veggies, visit your neighborhood food markets. These ingredients can be used to make your own vegetarian or vegan meals, whether you're camping out or having a picnic on the beach.

5. The employees at restaurants should be informed of your dietary choices when you dine there. A lot of restaurants are open to changing menu items to accommodate vegetarians and vegans.

6. Italian cuisine is influenced by Rastafarian culture and is frequently vegetarian or vegan. Look for it. There are likely to be foods like "Ital Stew" cooked with spices, beans, and veggies.

7. Plant-Based recipes: Vegetarian or vegan versions of many Caribbean recipes are readily available. For instance, you can ask for "Jerk Tofu" to replace the meat or a "Roti" loaded with vegetables.

8. Explore the various international cuisines that are served on the islands. Restaurants in the Middle East,

India, and Asia frequently provide vegetarian and vegan options, such as falafel, curries, and vegetable stir-fries.

Your dietary requirements can still be met with a little planning and discussion, even though vegetarian and vegan options might not be as common as seafood and animal dishes. While visiting St. Kitts and Nevis, you can eat a variety of delectable plant-based meals with a little amount of research and flexibility.

3.5 Rum Tastings and Traditional Beverages

In St. Kitts and Nevis, where rum manufacturing has a long history and the climate is tropical, traditional beverages and rum tastings are an important element of the cultural experience. Here is a detailed breakdown of the traditional beverages and rum tastings you can have while there:

1. Rum: Rum is the traditional Caribbean alcoholic beverage, and St. Kitts and Nevis both have a long

history of rum production. The islands are proud to have their distilleries that produce premium rum. Take advantage of the chance to partake in rum tastings at these distilleries to try a variety of rum flavors, from spiced and flavored rums to aged and dark variants. Visit St. Kitts Distillers and Brinley Gold Shipwreck Rum distilleries, among others.

2. Rum Punch is a popular drink in the Caribbean and something you should try while there. Typically, it consists of rum, grenadine syrup, spices, and fruit juices—often pineapple, orange, and lime. Make sure to sample this traditional drink at many establishments because each bartender may have their special spin on it.

3. Ting with a Sting: This cool beverage blends rum and locally produced Ting grapefruit soda. It's a delicious and zingy mixture that would be ideal to enjoy on a hot day.

4. Mauby: A traditional Caribbean drink prepared from the mauby tree's bark. It is frequently used as a

non-alcoholic choice and has a distinctive bittersweet flavor. For further complexity, some varieties do, however, include a tiny bit of rum.

5. Local fruit juices are very reviving and produced on St. Kitts and Nevis are a variety of tropical fruits. Enjoy exotic flavors like guava, passion fruit, and soursop either alone or in enticing fruit punches.

6. A common Caribbean beverage called sorrel is created from the hibiscus flower's petals. It can be enjoyed with or without rum during the Christmas season and is typically prepared as a festive beverage.

7. While rum reigns supreme, certain regional microbreweries are producing small-batch beers with distinctive characteristics. If you're a beer enthusiast, these beers are worth trying because they frequently contain ingredients with a Caribbean influence.

8. Coconut Water: In St. Kitts and Nevis, you may easily find fresh coconut water. Enjoy the mild sweetness and

natural hydration of this tropical treat, or treat yourself to "Coconut Water with a Kick" by drizzling a little rum in it.

9. Ginger Beer: A spicy and energizing non-alcoholic beverage is ginger beer. It's frequently consumed on its own or as a cocktail mixer.

10. Bush Tea: Bush tea is a calming herbal infusion produced from plants and herbs that are growing nearby. Although it isn't alcoholic, it is a vital component of island culture and is thought to provide several health advantages.

11. "Yellow Man" is a distinctive local beverage that blends rum and sweetened condensed milk. It's a decadent dessert that's frequently consumed on special occasions.

Several of the most well-known rum distilleries are:

1. The oldest rum distillery in the Caribbean is Mount Gay Rum Distillery, which is situated in St. Kitts.

2. Nevis Rum Distillery: This Nevis-based distillery is well-known for its velvety, mellow rums.

3. The St. Kitts-based Coral Bay Rum Distillery is renowned for its inventive rums, including its chocolate rum and its coffee rum.

4. Nightlife And Restaurants

4.1 Restaurants with Fine Dining

St. Kitts and Nevis are not only places for relaxation and adventure but also for gastronomic excellence because of their breathtaking natural beauty and rich culture. The islands provide a variety of gourmet dining options for people looking for an exquisite culinary experience in a classy setting. Here, we examine some of St. Kitts & Nevis's best restaurants for gourmet dining.

1. The Old Fig Tree Inn is a fine dining establishment with a Caribbean flair that is situated in Basseterre, St. Kitts. On the menu are items like grilled lobster with mango salsa and roasted chicken with sweet potato puree that are prepared with fresh, regional ingredients.

2. The Verandah is a restaurant with breathtaking views of the Caribbean Sea that is part of the Four Seasons Resort Nevis. The menu offers traditional Caribbean

cuisine with a contemporary touch, like shellfish risotto and jerk chicken with plantain mash.

3. Unexpected: This charming fine dining establishment is situated in Basseterre, St. Kitts. The menu offers dishes crafted with seasonal, fresh ingredients including black truffle risotto and foie gras-roasted duck breast.

4. Spice Mill Restaurant is a Caribbean fine dining establishment with a location in New Castle, St. Kitts. The menu offers dishes crafted using typical Caribbean ingredients, like conch fritters and goat curry on roti.

5. The Dining Room at the Marriott Resort is a sophisticated dining establishment with a view of the Caribbean Sea that is part of the Marriott Resort St. Kitts. The menu offers traditional American fare including lobster mac & cheese and filet mignon with béarnaise sauce.

6. The Great House Restaurant in St. Kitts offers a dining experience that combines Caribbean flavors with

global influences. It is housed in the venerable Ottley's Plantation Inn. Dine on the balcony that overlooks the lovely grounds or in the Great House from the 18th century. The wine list nicely matches the menu's culinary offerings, which include meals made with locally produced products.

7. The Pavilion at Christophe Harbour (St. Kitts)*: The Pavilion is renowned for its upmarket dining experience and is located at the exclusive Christophe Harbour. Fresh seafood, steaks, and meals with a Caribbean flair are included on the menu at the restaurant, which has sweeping views of the Caribbean Sea. The classy atmosphere makes it a great option for special gatherings.

8. The Mill (Nevis) is a renowned fine dining institution that is housed in an 18th-century sugar mill at Montpelier Plantation & Beach. The restaurant's menu combines Caribbean and Mediterranean flavors and features creative meals made using ingredients that are

grown nearby. Couples frequently choose it because of the enchanting environment and friendly service.

9. Ottley's Plantation Inn (St. Kitts): Ottley's Plantation Inn provides visitors with The Royal Palm Restaurant in addition to The Great House Restaurant. This outdoor restaurant specializes in contemporary Caribbean food with an emphasis on farm-to-table ingredients. Excellent service and a charming plantation setting make for a wonderful eating experience.

10. At the Park Hyatt St. Kitts, Coral Grill (St. Kitts) provides a classy dining experience. Guests can observe the cooks at work in the restaurant's open kitchen. Local foods, premium steaks, and fresh seafood are highlighted on the menu. It's a great option for wine connoisseurs because the extensive wine selection matches the culinary options.

11. Nevis' Coconut Grove, which is known for its beachside restaurants, is located on Pinney's Beach. The restaurant has a broad menu with an emphasis on local

cuisine, Caribbean delicacies, and other cuisines. A special touch is added to the dinner by eating with your toes on the beach and listening to the waves.

12. Bananas Restaurant (Nevis)*: This lovely Charlestown, Nevis restaurant is renowned for its cozy atmosphere and inventive fare. The menu at Bananas Restaurant features a fusion of Caribbean and international tastes and is periodically updated to highlight local, seasonal products. The wide selection of wines and the kind of service improve the overall eating experience.

4.2 Casual Restaurants and Beachfront Eateries

Along with its upscale restaurants, St. Kitts and Nevis has a thriving scene of beachside eateries and informal dining facilities where you may savor delectable meals in a laid-back and attractive environment. Here are some of these seaside and casual eating options in more detail:

1. Reggae Beach Bar & Grill is a casual dining establishment with a beachside environment that is situated in Frigate Bay, St. Kitts. Caribbean cuisine is offered on the menu, including jerk chicken and fish tacos.

2. The Boathouse is a casual dining establishment with a waterfront backdrop that is located in Nevis. The menu offers seafood meals including lobster bisque and grilled mahi-mahi.

3. The Palms Court Gardens & Restaurant is a casual eating establishment with a garden setting that is part of the St. Kitts Marriott Resort. American cuisine is offered on the menu, including burgers and pasta meals.

4. The Old Tavern is a casual dining establishment with a historic setting that is situated in Basseterre, St. Kitts. The menu offers classic Caribbean fare like roti, bakes, and saltfish.

5. The Sunset Grill is a casual dining establishment with a view of the sunset that is situated in Nevis. Caribbean cuisine is offered on the menu, including grilled fish and chicken wings.

6. On the outskirts of Christophe Harbour Marina in St. Kitts, Salt Plage provides a casual yet elegant eating environment with breathtaking sunset views. Caribbean and Mediterranean flavors are combined on the menu, and there is a sizable drink menu.

7. Known for its delicious beverages, prime beachside position, and live music, Double Deuce is a popular beach bar and restaurant on Nevis. It's a well-liked location to eat informally and take in the Nevian ambiance.

8. Shiggidy Shack (St. Kitts): Located on South Friars Beach, Shiggidy Shack is a beautiful beach bar and grill. Due to its welcoming service and delicious seafood meals, it is popular among both locals and tourists. A

laid-back atmosphere is created by the rustic decor and seats on the beach.

9. Restaurant at Oualie Beach Resort in Nevis: The restaurant at Oualie Beach Resort provides beachside dining with a focus on fresh seafood and international cuisine. It's a great spot to relax and take in the tranquil beach atmosphere of Nevis.

10. Nevis' LION ROCK BEACH BAR & GRILL is well-known for its seafood and regional specialties, like as conch fritters and grilled fish. You can eat there informally while putting your toes in the sand.

11. St. Kitts' Shipwreck Beach Bar & Grill is a beachside treasure with a laid-back ambiance, as the name of the establishment suggests. There are traditional Caribbean dishes on the menu, and it's a great spot to enjoy cocktails while the sun sets.

12. Nevis' Chevy's Calypso Beach Bar & Grill serves a fusion of Mexican and Caribbean food. While dining,

visitors can take in Pinney's Beach's turquoise waves while savoring tacos, burritos, and other Tex-Mex fare.

4.3 Bars and Nightclubs

St. Kitts and Nevis are renowned for their tranquil beaches and stunning scenery, but they also have a thriving nightlife culture that welcomes both locals and tourists. On these Caribbean islands, nightclubs and bars offer the ideal atmosphere for unwinding, dancing to upbeat music, and savoring a choice of drinks. Here is a detailed look at St. Kitts and Nevis's nightlife options:

1. On St. Kitts' renowned South Frigate Bay Beach, Vibes Beach Bar is a well-liked destination for both daytime leisure and evening entertainment. The seaside location is ideal for watching the sunset, and as the night wears on, the bar comes to life with DJ performances, live music, and stargazing.

2. Mr. X's Shiggidy Shack in St. Kitts is renowned for its laid-back and fun-loving atmosphere. It is located on

Frigate Bay Beach. The "Killer Bee" cocktail, a strong concoction that has become legendary among tourists, is the claim to fame of this beach bar. The party frequently lasts well into the night thanks to live music and DJ performances.

3. Boozies on the Beach (Nevis): Boozies on the Beach is a beach bar with a relaxed ambiance that is situated on Pinney's Beach in Nevis. It's a fantastic location for watching the sunset while sipping beverages and listening to live music. The bar frequently features local artists and bands, resulting in a calm yet energetic atmosphere.

4. The Dock (St. Kitts): The Dock, a popular destination for nightlife in St. Kitts, is tucked away in the center of Basseterre and features a blend of Caribbean and international music. The bar offers a wide selection of beverages, from regional beers to inventive cocktails, and the roomy outside atmosphere is ideal for dancing.

5. Sunshines Beach Bar (Nevis): Situated on Nevis' Pinney's Beach, Sunshines Beach Bar is renowned for its delectable "Killer Bee" cocktail and its friendly ambiance. The pub frequently features live reggae bands, fostering a peaceful and comfortable atmosphere for visitors to experience the island spirit.

6. South Friars Beach Bar (St. Kitts): During the day, South Friars Beach Bar offers a serene seaside environment, but at night, it comes alive. For its seafood meals, beverages, and live entertainment, it is a favorite of both locals and tourists. The pub frequently offers DJ nights and themed parties.

7. Monkey Bar (Nevis): This luxury nightlife establishment is located within the Four Seasons Resort Nevis. Craft beverages, a stylish lounge space, and occasionally scheduled DJ or live music acts are all included. The setting is ideal for those seeking a chic night out on Nevis.

8. Ziggy's (St. Kitts): Ziggy's is a well-liked nightclub with a lively dance floor and DJ set that is situated on the Frigate Bay Strip in St. Kitts. The club conducts themed events and parties, making it a popular destination for anyone looking for a fun night of dancing and mingling.

9. Nevis' Oualie Beach pub is a laid-back beachfront pub with live music, frequently performed by local musicians. It's the perfect spot to unwind while holding a beverage, taking in the sea breeze, and listening to calming music.

10. DJ Outlet is a nightclub in St. Kitts that features DJs spinning a range of EDM genres for individuals who prefer electronic dance music. For fans of electronic music and late-night dancing, it's a fantastic alternative.

11. The Royal Beach Casino has a nightclub that is open every day from 10 p.m. to 2 a.m. The nightclub offers table games, slot machines, live DJs, and live music.

12. The Boathouse: This restaurant also includes a late-night bar with live entertainment and DJs. After dinner, the bar is a fantastic spot to unwind with a drink and some music.

4.4 Entertainment and Live Music

Although St. Kitts and Nevis are renowned for their serene beaches and green surroundings, the islands come alive at night with the sounds of live music and enthralling entertainment. You'll discover a rich tapestry of live performances and entertainment alternatives to enjoy throughout your vacation, whether you're a music enthusiast, a culture seeker, or just trying to unwind.

1. The Sugar Factory: This establishment is situated in Basseterre, St. Kitts, and offers a range of live music, including reggae, jazz, and blues. A restaurant and bar are also located there.

2. The Limelight Lounge, a venue in Frigate Bay, St. Kitts, hosts live performances by regional and

international musicians. A restaurant and bar are also located there.

3. This restaurant's bar, The Old Tavern, features live music on the weekends. The bar is a nice location to unwind with a drink while listening to regional music from the Caribbean.

4. The Nevis Performing Arts Centre is a performance space in Charlestown, Nevis that regularly stages theater, dance, and musical productions.

5. The Cultural Center: This location, which is also in Charlestown, Nevis, also holds a range of cultural activities like seminars and festivals.

6. Steel Pan Music: The steel pan, often known as the steel drum, is a well-known instrument throughout the Caribbean. It creates rhythmic and melodic music that immediately takes you to the islands. Local steel pan bands frequently play at beachside bars, eateries, and

cultural gatherings. Your evenings will have a little Caribbean flair thanks to their upbeat performances.

7. Calypso & Soca: These musical styles, which are essential to Caribbean culture, can be enjoyed while you're there. These upbeat and contagious rhythms are routinely performed by local musicians and bands at a variety of locations, giving your nights a lively soundtrack.

8. Reggae and Dancehall: St. Kitts and Nevis has a devoted fan base for both genres of music. These Jamaican-influenced beats can be grooved to at nightclubs, music festivals, and beachside bars. Watch for live reggae performances by both local and touring performers.

9. Live Bands and Solo Artists: Numerous pubs and eateries have live bands and solo performers that perform in a variety of musical genres, including jazz, blues, pop, and rock. These shows provide a variety of

musical experiences, which you may take in while indulging in regional cuisine or sipping beverages.

10. Beach bonfires: A few seaside businesses have bonfires on the sand while acoustic music is played. It's a calm, cozy atmosphere where you may listen to the steel pan or guitar while admiring the magnificent Caribbean sky.

11. Karaoke Nights: Seek out clubs that conduct karaoke nights if you're in the mood for some participatory entertainment. It's a wonderful opportunity to demonstrate your singing prowess or just take in the interesting performances of other audience members.

St. Kitts and Nevis provide a wide variety of live music and entertainment alternatives, whether you prefer the lulling rhythms of dancehall in a lively nightclub or the calming melodies of steel pan music by the beach.

5. Shopping

5.1 Locally Made Crafts and Art

With numerous local artists and craftspeople producing exquisite pieces of art, St. Kitts and Nevis boasts a thriving arts and crafts community. The following are some of the most well-liked regional crafts:

1. Wax resist is used to color fabric using the batik technique. Batik is frequently used to make elaborate and bright designs.

2. Pottery is a traditional craft that has been carried out for centuries on St. Kitts & Nevis. In addition to producing aesthetic objects like figures and vases, pottery is frequently used to produce useful items like bowls and cups.

3. Woodcarving is a craft that may be used to make a wide range of items, including furniture and figures.

Local wildlife and vegetation are frequently portrayed in wood carving.

4. Jewelry is a widely purchased souvenir in St. Kitts and Nevis. Coral and seashells are two common native resources used to make jewelry.

5. Textiles manufactured by hand include woven baskets, straw hats, and clothes with embroidery.

6. Coconut-Related items: The Caribbean is home to an abundance of coconuts, and a variety of coconut-based items may be found there. Look for coconut soaps, coconut oil, and even pastries and candies that contain coconut.

In St. Kitts and Nevis, you may find regional artwork and handicrafts in several locations, including:

1. The Artisan Village is a neighborhood in Romney Manor, St. Kitts, which several regional artists and craftspeople call home.

2. Many hotels in St. Kitts and Nevis have gift stores where guests can purchase items made locally.

3. Additionally, some duty-free shops are selling regional artwork and handicrafts at the airport.

5.2 Duty-Free Shopping

As a duty-free port, St. Kitts and Nevis allows you to buy a wide range of products without paying taxes. The following are some of the top-selling duty-free products:

1. Liquor, beer, and wine all fall under the category of alcohol.

2. Cigarettes, cigars, and pipe tobacco are all considered to be tobacco products.

3. Men's and women's fragrances are both considered to be perfumes.

4. Cameras, laptops, and tablets are all examples of electronics.

5. Men's and women's apparel, as well as accessories, are included in this category.

In St. Kitts and Nevis, duty-free shops can be found in several locations, including:

1. The airport: Before and after you pass through customs, there are a variety of duty-free stores at the airport.

2. The cruise ship docks: The cruise ship docks also have a variety of duty-free businesses.

3. The larger retail centers: These centers, including the Bayside Centre in Basseterre, St. Kitts, offer some duty-free businesses.

It's crucial to be aware of the restrictions on what you can bring back to your country when shopping for things at duty-free stores.

5.3 Boutiques and Souvenir Shops

In addition to duty-free shops, St. Kitts & Nevis has a large number of boutiques and souvenir stores where you may purchase a wide range of apparel, presents, and souvenirs. The following are some of the most well-known boutiques and gift shops:

1. The Craft Market is a wonderful location to find a variety of regional handicrafts as well as gifts including T-shirts, magnets, and key chains. It is situated in Basseterre, St. Kitts.

2. The Old Market Square, which is in Charlestown, Nevis, is a great area to find regional crafts and mementos.

3. The Bayside Centre is a shopping center with several gift shops, boutiques, and duty-free stores that are situated in Basseterre, St. Kitts.

4. The Frigate Bay Marina is a marina in St. Kitts with several gift shops, boutiques, dining establishments, and pubs.

5. The Nevis Botanical Gardens is a botanical garden in Nevis that features a small gift shop with things manufactured by regional makers.

5.4 Local Stores and Street Vendors

Visit the local markets and street vendors in St. Kitts and Nevis if you want a more genuine shopping experience. These markets are fantastic places to find local goods, fresh fruit, and mementos.

Local street sellers and markets that are particularly well-liked include:

1. The Basseterre Market is open every day and is situated in Basseterre, St. Kitts.

2. The Charlestown Market is open every day and is situated in Charlestown, Nevis.

3. The Old Road Market is open every Wednesday and Saturday and is situated at Old Road, St. Kitts.

4. Every Sunday afternoon, the Frigate Bay Marina hosts the Frigate Bay Vendors' Fair.

5. Every Saturday and Sunday, the Nevis Botanical Gardens hosts the Nevis Craft Fair.

6. Farmers' markets: On occasion, St. Kitts and Nevis hold farmers' markets when local producers and craftspeople congregate to display their wares. These markets are excellent places to buy fruits, vegetables, handmade items, and other organic products straight from the growers.

7. In addition to food markets, you can also discover craft markets where local artisans sell their wares like pottery, colorful textiles, and woven baskets. These markets provide a window into the artistic traditions of the islands.

8. Street sellers frequently line the streets of well-known tourist destinations, selling a variety of goods and keepsakes. These sellers sell items with island themes, including jewelry, clothes, and regional art.

It's crucial to understand the culture of haggling when shopping at neighborhood markets and on the street. Do not be scared to bargain; it is usual to wrangle over the price of products.

6. Top Attractions You Must Visit

6.1 National Park at Brimstone Hill Fortress

On the island of St. Kitts, Brimstone Hill Fortress National Park serves as a striking example of the island's illustrious past and impressive architectural prowess. For history buffs and anybody interested in learning more about the colonial past of the Caribbean, a trip to this UNESCO World Heritage Site is essential.

The stronghold, which is perched atop a massive volcanic hill, provides stunning 360-degree views of the ocean below. The stronghold itself is an engineering masterpiece from the 18th century that demonstrates the British colonial forces' strategic thinking. With its imposing stone walls, intact cannons, and detailed embellishments, it offers an enthralling look into the island's past.

The fortress's well-preserved barracks, officer's quarters, and majestic citadel make for a fascinating voyage through time. The fortress's museum provides a fuller understanding of its past, including its part in colonial warfare in the Caribbean and the lives of individuals who served there.

Brimstone Hill is a special fusion of natural beauty and cultural history since, in addition to its historical value, it is surrounded by lush foliage and fauna. Hikers can explore the fortress's pathways and come across unique plants and animals.

In addition to being a popular tourist destination, Brimstone Hill Fortress National Park serves as a living memorial to the fortitude and inventiveness of those who constructed it.

6.2 The Scenic Railway in St. Kitts

A one-of-a-kind adventure, the St. Kitts Scenic Railway takes you through the gorgeous interior and shoreline of

St. Kitts. It offers a distinctive method to discover the island's natural beauty and is a living remnant of the island's past as a center for the sugar industry.

The railway, often known as the "Sugar Train," provides a relaxing ride around the entire island on a 30-mile track. You'll be treated to breathtaking views of luscious rainforests, rolling hills, quaint villages, and the glittering Caribbean Sea as you set out on this beautiful excursion. The open-air railcars provide unobstructed views that are ideal for taking pictures and taking in the surroundings.

The history of St. Kitts, including its sugar plantations, colonial past, and the influence of the railway on the island's development, is fascinatingly revealed during a narrated tour. Additionally, vivid narratives and legends are told to passengers, adding a great storytelling component to the trip.

One of the highlights of the journey is a stop at the "Last Railway Station," where visitors may tour a former sugar estate with intact machinery and verdant gardens. You'll develop a deeper understanding of the sugar industry on the island and how it affects the way of life there.

The St. Kitts Scenic Railway is more than simply a trip on the rails; it's a fascinating immersion into the history and beauty of the island. It's a memorable trip that brings together history, culture, and stunning landscapes.

6.3 Hike to Nevis Peak

Nevis Peak Hike gives intrepid visitors the chance to ascend the dormant volcano that rises 3,232 feet (985 meters) above sea level as the highest point on the island of Nevis. This strenuous walk rewards you with stunning panoramic views of Nevis and the nearby islands as well as beautiful rainforests and cloud forests.

The trip starts in the quaint town of Jessups and gradually climbs through thick woodland. You'll come across a variety of flora and fauna, including tropical birds and unusual plants, along the trip. Sturdy hiking boots are required because the trail can be steep and muddy despite being well-marked.

As you climb, the air gets drier and more humid, signaling that you are getting close to the cloud forest. This distinct habitat is shrouded in mist and has unusual ferns and moss-covered trees. It's a bizarre experience that makes you feel as though you've entered another world.

The hike's steep ascent up the volcano's cone, which is its final leg, can be physically taxing but is well worth it. Awe-inspiring vistas of the entire island, neighboring St. Kitts, and the broad Caribbean Sea await you at the summit.

For experienced hikers in good physical condition, the Nevis Peak Hike is a strenuous excursion. It's a chance to get in touch with nature, push yourself, and take in some of the Caribbean's most spectacular views.

6.4 Pinney's Beach

On the picture-perfect island of Nevis, Pinney's Beach is a picture-perfect expanse of golden sand that personifies the Caribbean dream. Visitors will find peace and comfort at this unspoiled beach, a peaceful paradise where blue seas lazily lap the shore.

Pinney's Beach stands out due to its pristine beauty and somewhat remote location. In contrast to some of the Caribbean's busier beaches, Pinney's maintains a tranquil and genuine atmosphere. There are beachside eateries and pubs with thatched roofs where you may enjoy delectable seafood, refreshing drinks, and friendly Nevisian friendliness.

There are numerous water sports and activities available at the beach. There are many possibilities to discover Nevis's marine life and natural beauty, from snorkeling among vibrant coral reefs to kayaking along the coast.

The breathtaking view of Nevis Peak, the island's dormant volcano, which serves as a dramatic background to the sunsets that paint the sky in hues of orange and pink, is one of Pinney's Beach's most recognizable characteristics.

Pinney's Beach offers a unique Caribbean experience, whether you're looking for leisure, water sports, or a romantic getaway. It's a location where the pace of time seems to slow down and the magnificence of nature is highlighted.

6.5 Historic Basseterre District

The oldest continuously inhabited European settlement in the Caribbean and a UNESCO World Heritage Site is Basseterre. The area is in Basseterre's capital city and is home to several historic structures, including:

-***The Circus:** One of Basseterre's most recognizable landmarks is a roundabout that was constructed in the 18th century.

-***Government House:** This stunning Georgian-style building serves as the Governor-General of St. Kitts and Nevis's official residence.

-***Parliament Building:** The St. Kitts and Nevis Parliament is housed in this 19th-century structure.

- * **Fort Charles:** The city's defenses were bolstered by the construction of this fort in the 17th century.

-* **St. The oldest Anglican church in the Caribbean is George's Anglican Church, which was constructed in the 18th century.

6.6 Caribelle Batik

In Basseterre, St. Kitts, there is a batik factory and workshop called Caribelle Batik. The firm, one of the oldest and most renowned batik companies in the Caribbean, was established in 1971 by Barbara Anderson.

Clothing, home decor, and souvenirs are just a few of the many batik products made by Caribelle Batik. Local artists hand-paint the batik while employing traditional Indonesian methods to create it.

Visitors to the facility can take advantage of a choice of tours and workshops to learn more about the creation of batiks. The excursions are a fantastic chance to discover the batik's history, culture, and manufacturing process.

6.7 Romney Manor

In St. Kitts, there is an old sugar plantation called Romney Manor. The manor home was constructed in the 18th century and is a stunning illustration of Georgian design. Publicly accessible lawns and gardens encircle the manor house.

The manor house is now a museum with items from the time of the plantations on display. Additionally, there is a restaurant on the property that provides regional Caribbean food.

The Romney Manor Estate, a well-liked tourist destination, is where the manor house is situated. A rum distillery, a botanical garden, and a nature walk are located on the site.

6.8 Timothy Hill

In St. Kitts, there is a viewpoint called Timothy Hill Overlook. The overlook provides breathtaking views of the neighboring island of Nevis, the Caribbean Sea, and the mountains in the area.

The viewpoint is accessible to the general public and is situated on the Romney Manor Estate. At the overlook, there is a tiny parking area from which a short distance leads to the viewpoint.

Timothy Hill Overlook is best visited early in the day or late in the day when the sun is not as intense. The overlook is a wonderful spot to unwind and take in the scenery.

At Timothy Hill Overlook, you may also accomplish the following:

-* Climb the hill for even better views: There is a short trek to the top of the hill.

-* Enjoy a picnic: A small picnic space is available at the overlook for your use.

-* Snap pictures: Bring your camera since the views from Timothy Hill Overlook are just breathtaking.

-* Unwind and take in the views: The overlook is a fantastic location to unwind and take in the sights.

6.9 Black Rocks

On St. Kitts' northern coast is Black Rocks, a natural marvel that displays the unadulterated beauty of volcanic structures. The Caribbean Sea's turquoise waves and the black, angular rocks that make up this natural wonder make for an eye-catching contrast.

The location, which features spectacular basalt rocks carved by nature over millions of years, is proof of the island's volcanic origins. The pounding waves and stunning seascape created by the cliffs give the image a sense of excitement.

Visitors can explore Black Rocks on foot, climbing over the rocky formations and admiring the breathtaking views of the nearby shoreline. It's a well-liked location for photography because the stark contrast between the deep-blue water, light-colored rocks, and thick foliage makes for an arresting background.

Black Rocks is a rare opportunity to observe St. Kitts' geological history in a dramatic and scenic setting, even though swimming there might not be advised due to the strong currents and rocky terrain. Nature lovers and anyone looking to connect with the island's natural marvels must go there.

6.10 Alexander Hamilton House

One of the founding fathers of the United States, Alexander Hamilton, was born in the Alexander Hamilton House, which is situated on the lovely island of Nevis. This historic home, also known as the Hamilton Museum, takes tourists on a fascinating historical tour that focuses on Alexander Hamilton's life and contributions to society.

-**Alexander Hamilton's Birthplace**: Alexander Hamilton was born in 1757 at the Alexander Hamilton House. The home is a two-story Georgian-style building that has undergone painstaking restoration to accurately depict the time when Hamilton resided there. It is a real artifact from American history.

-** Museum Exhibits**: Alexander Hamilton's life, career, and accomplishments in the United States are all highlighted in the house's current role as a museum. Visitors can examine antiques, records, and interactive exhibits that shed light on Hamilton's formative years on

Nevis and his eventual contribution to the development of the country's financial system.

-** Hamilton's Nevisian Roots:** Nevis was important to Alexander Hamilton's early development. His Nevisian background, his education on the island, and how these experiences shaped his political and economic beliefs are all covered in the museum.

-**Teaching Experience**: The Alexander Hamilton House is a useful teaching tool that clarifies the ties between Nevis and the United States throughout history. It provides a greater appreciation of the character who inspired the famous image and the values he upheld.

-**Gardens and Grounds**: The museum is surrounded by exquisitely planted gardens that give visitors a serene and lovely setting. It's a peaceful location to consider the historical significance of the location and take in Nevis's natural beauty.

-** Cultural tradition**: The museum highlights Nevisian culture and tradition in addition to Alexander Hamilton. It displays the island's heritage, customs, and contributions to the global community.

-**Visitor Experience**: At the Alexander Hamilton House, guests can anticipate a knowledgeable tour guide who will share a wealth of knowledge about Hamilton's life, his relationship to Nevis, and the larger historical backdrop. The educated tour guides tell interesting stories that vividly depict history.

- The home is situated in a beautiful area with views of the Caribbean Sea in Charlestown, Nevis. For visitors who want to learn more about the island's rich history, it is ideally located close to other historical monuments and tourist destinations.

-**Preserving History**: The Alexander Hamilton House's repair and preservation efforts are admirable because they ensure that future generations will recognize the value of this historical site.

A voyage into the past, the Alexander Hamilton House offers a fuller understanding of the life and contributions of one of America's founding fathers. On the island of Nevis, history comes alive as the contributions of Alexander Hamilton are honored in a beautiful Caribbean environment.

6.11 Cockleshell Bay

Cockleshell Bay is a beautiful and undeveloped area of the Caribbean paradise, located at the southernmost point of St. Kitts. This serene beach is well known for its fine white sands, clean waters, and breathtaking views of Nevis Peak on the other side of the narrows.

-**Secluded Beauty**: In contrast to other Caribbean beaches that are busier, Cockleshell Bay provides a tranquil haven. It's the perfect location for people looking for peace, tranquility, and a sense of connection with nature.

-**Water Adventures**: Cockleshell Bay's serene and inviting waters are ideal for swimming and snorkeling. You can explore the colorful marine life-filled coral reefs' lively underwater habitat.

-**Beachfront Dining**: There are several quaint beach bars and eateries along the shore where you can relish mouthwatering Caribbean fare and swig tropical drinks. A remarkable experience is eating when your toes are in the sand and listening to the soft lapping of the waves.

- The breathtaking view of Nevis, which is only a short boat ride away, is one of the highlights of Cockleshell Bay. For beachgoers, Nevis Peak's abrupt ascent from the water makes for a beautiful background.

-** Water Sports**: Risk-takers can engage in activities like jet skiing, kayaking, and paddleboarding on the water. Rental gear is easily accessible, enabling you to maximize your time on the water.

-** Sunset Serenity**: Cockleshell Bay is renowned for its mesmerizing sunsets. The sky becomes a canvas of vibrant colors as the sun sets below the horizon, evoking a beautiful and peaceful environment.

-**Nature and species**: The region's natural beauty is abundant, and you might come across species like sea turtles and tropical birds. The bay is a component of a marine park that is protected, conserving its pristine surroundings.

Cockleshell Bay epitomizes a peaceful Caribbean vacation. This picturesque location on St. Kitts guarantees a tranquil and wonderful experience, whether you're relaxing on the beach, snorkeling in the clear waters, or eating beachside.

6.12 Frigate Bay

On the island of St. Kitts, Frigate Bay is a mesmerizing location that provides the ideal fusion of scenic beauty, aquatic activities, and a buzzing nightlife. This beautiful bay, which is divided into North Frigate Bay and South Frigate Bay, has grown to be a well-liked destination for both tourists and locals.

- Frigate Bay is home to exquisite golden beaches that extend down the coastline and provide beachgoers with an attractive backdrop. The Caribbean Sea's calm, clear waters are excellent for swimming, and its mild waves make it a great location for water sports.

-**Water Activities**: Frigate Bay offers a variety of water activities for explorers of all skill levels, including jet skiing, paddleboarding, snorkeling, and sailing. You may easily discover St. Kitts' maritime treasures by renting equipment and going on guided tours.

-*" South Frigate Bay**: This neighborhood is well known for its seaside bars and eateries. You may enjoy live music, Caribbean cuisine, and tropical drinks in this bustling location. The beach bars frequently hold events and gatherings, fostering a lively nightlife.

- North Frigate Bay, in comparison, is a little more serene and perfect for people seeking peace. It's a wonderful place to unwind and enjoy the sunshine while surrounded by waving palm trees.

-**Cockleshell Bay Excursions**: From Frigate Bay, it's simple to get to Cockleshell Bay, which is close by and famous for its breathtaking sunsets and water activities. Take a quick boat ride to the lovely island of Nevis to discover its historical attractions and pristine beaches.

-**Scenic Views**: From Frigate Bay, the vista of Nevis Peak is nothing short of magnificent. The famous volcano rises majestically across the passageways, providing a picture-perfect background that enhances the allure of the harbor.

-**Golfing**: The Royal St. Kitts Golf Club, which is close to Frigate Bay, will be appreciated by golfers. This championship golf course has breathtaking Caribbean Sea views along with difficult fairways set within lush tropical surroundings.

-**Cultural Experiences**: Frigate Bay offers opportunities to experience local culture away from the shore. Discover the adjacent towns, indulge in some regional food, and converse with the welcoming inhabitants who are happy to explain the island's history and customs.

Frigate Bay is ideally situated close to Basseterre, the island's capital, and the Robert L. Bradshaw International Airport, making it accessible for visitors arriving by ship or aircraft.

Frigate Bay is a must-visit location on St. Kitts because of its distinctive blend of natural beauty, water activities, exciting nightlife, and cultural experiences. Frigate Bay has everything you're looking for in one alluring location, whether you're looking for adventure, relaxation, or a taste of Caribbean culture.

7. Visits to Nevis Island

7.1 Charlestown and Nevis's Historic Sites

Nevis' lovely capital, Charlestown, is a picturesque Caribbean city with a rich history and a bevy of protected historical landmarks. Cobblestone streets, Georgian-style architecture, and a rich cultural past come together to create a compelling ambiance, offering visitors a lovely trip back in time.

-**Exploring Charlestown**: The bustling streets packed with vibrant buildings, neighborhood stores, and lively markets are what define Charlestown's core. It's a location where you can become fully immersed in Nevis's dynamic culture and take in the town's distinctive fusion of colonial and Caribbean influences.

-**Alexander Hamilton's Birthplace**: Alexander Hamilton, one of the founding fathers of America, was born in Charlestown, making it one of the city's most important historic sites. You can learn more about the life and formative years of this great person by visiting the Alexander Hamilton House, which is now a museum.

-**St. One of the earliest Anglican churches in the Caribbean is George's Anglican Church, which was erected in 1670. Its historic graveyard and whitewashed facade offer a window into the island's colonial past.

-**The Museum of Nevis History**: This museum provides a thorough account of Nevis's history, including its indigenous roots, colonial era, and the impact of the sugar industry. It is housed in an 18th-century Georgian-style edifice.

-**Charlestown Waterfront**: Charlestown's waterfront is home to a picturesque promenade where visitors may stroll along the beach, take in the view of Nevis Peak, and observe ferries traveling between Nevis and St. Kitts. It's a serene setting where you can unwind and take in the scenery.

- The Bath Hotel, a once-famous resort from the Georgian era, is now in ruins yet nonetheless exudes an aura of fading grandeur. The Bath Spring House, which lies nearby, still offers samples of the island's naturally heated volcanic spring water, which is thought to have therapeutic powers.

-** Horatio Nelson Museum**: This museum honors Admiral Horatio Nelson, a well-known British naval officer who wed a Nevisian woman named Fanny Nisbet on Nevis in 1787. Objects and displays from Nelson's life and relationship to the island are on display at the museum.

-**Charlestown Market**: The neighborhood market in Charlestown is a bustling setting where you may observe Nevisians going about their daily lives. Fresh food, spices, handicrafts, and souvenirs are all sold by vendors. It's the perfect place to meet locals and try genuine Nevisian food.

-**Cultural activities**: Depending on when you visit, you could have the chance to take part in festivals and activities that highlight Nevisian customs, music, and food. These occasions frequently occur in and around Charlestown.

-**Historic Walking Tour**: To properly experience Charlestown's historic charm, think about joining a tour guide for a walking excursion. You will be escorted by knowledgeable guides who will share fascinating anecdotes and insights about the town's features and history as they show you around.

-**Shopping and Dining**: There are many stores in Charlestown where you can buy regional handicrafts, trinkets, and spices. Street food vendors to upscale restaurants serving Caribbean and foreign cuisine are all options for dining.

An in-depth understanding of Nevis's history and its impact on the rest of the globe can be gained by visiting Charlestown and its historic sites, which offer an enthralling window into the past. It's a location where contemporary Caribbean hospitality meets old-world charm, making it a crucial visit for anybody touring this magical island.

7.2 Nevis Botanical Gardens

The tranquil Caribbean island of Nevis is home to the Botanical Gardens of Nevis, sometimes known as the "Garden of Eden," which is a horticultural haven. These gardens, which are a lush and colorful refuge at the foot of Nevis Peak, highlight the varied flora of the Caribbean and beyond.

- The Nevis Botanical Gardens are a labor of love that has been painstakingly created and cared for to highlight the island's natural beauty. Visitors are taken on a sensory tour through themed gardens, each of which has a distinct personality.

- The gardens are famed for its beautiful orchid terraces, where a magnificent variety of orchid species bloom in riotous colors. A photographer's paradise, these terraces are enhanced by the fragrant flowers.

-** Palm Walk**: Stroll along this shady boulevard that is bordered by imposing royal palm trees. A pleasant environment for thought and relaxation is created by the calm atmosphere and the soft rustling of the palm leaves.

- Enter the Jungle Conservatory to experience a verdant utopia that perfectly captures the luxuriance of a tropical jungle. Exotic plants, colorful butterflies, and even a resident parrot can all be found here.

- With its Zen-like atmosphere, the Asian Garden transports you to the Far East. It has a koi pond, bamboo groves, and beautiful landscaping with Asian influences that exude calm and balance.

-**Medicinal Herb Garden**: In the medicinal herb garden, learn the secrets of conventional herbal therapies. Discover the medicinal benefits of several plants and their traditional uses in Caribbean and international medicine.

- The bamboo garden displays the variety and adaptability of several bamboo species. The peaceful environment brings out the beauty and practicality of this extraordinary plant.

-** Tropical Fruit Trees**: A wide variety of tropical fruit trees, including mangoes, citrus, avocados, and others, can be found in the gardens. You might be able to try some of these delectable fruits depending on the season.

-** Sculptures and Art**: The gardens are filled with sculptures and artworks that blend in with the surrounding landscape. These creative aspects give the experience an additional dimension of beauty and originality.

- The Botanical Gardens of Nevis serves as a hub for education and conservation efforts in addition to being a beautiful location. To promote knowledge of plant diversity and environmental care, they provide seminars and workshops.

- You may find out more about the gardens' mission and the flora you'll see at its visitor center and gift shop. Books and souvenirs with a botanical theme can be found in the gift shop.

-**Events & Private Functions**: The gardens frequently serve as a venue for special occasions including weddings, theatrical productions, and garden tours. To see whether any special events coincide with your visit, check the schedule.

The Nevis Botanical Gardens offer a serene escape into the beauties of nature. These gardens on the lovely island of Nevis offer a sensory feast and a profound connection with the natural world, whether you're a plant expert, a nature lover, or just looking for a peaceful place to unwind.

7.3 Nelson's Spring & Hot Springs

On the island of Nevis, in the community of Bath, there is a natural hot spring known as Nelson's Spring and Hot Springs. The spring bears Horatio Nelson's name since it is believed that he took a bath there while he was a resident of Nevis.

The spring is concealed by dense vegetation and set in a remote area of the rainforest. The spring's pure, blue water is reputed to have medicinal qualities.

There is a nominal entrance fee and the spring is open to the public. On-site restrooms and showers are available.

At Nelson's Spring and Hot Springs, visitors can engage in a variety of activities, such as:

-* Take a springtime bath: The water in the spring is cozy and soothing. It is said to be beneficial for aching joints and muscles.

-* Swim in the pool: Next to the spring is a pool where you can go swimming.

-* Take a mud bath: Next to the spring, there is a mud bath where you can cover your skin with mud.

-* According to legend, the mud has cleansing qualities.

-* Get a massage: You can get a massage from the on-site massage therapist.

-* Unwind in the rainforest: The spring is tucked away in a remote area of the jungle. It's a wonderful location for unwinding and taking in Nevis's natural splendor.

7.4 Nevis Beaches

One of the nicest beaches in the Caribbean is found on the island of Nevis. The beaches' beautiful sand, crystal-clear water, and gentle waves are well-known for them.

Nevis has some of the top beaches in the world:

1. The most visited beach on Nevis, Pinney's Beach, is renowned for its tranquil seas and fine white sand. Hotels, eateries, and bars are all located along the shore.

2. Coral Beach: Situated on Nevis' west coast, this beach is well-known for its coral reefs and crystal-clear seas. Scuba diving and snorkeling enthusiasts frequently visit the beach.

3. The longest beach on Nevis is called Long Beach, and it is found on the island's east coast. The beach is well-known for having calm waves and is a favorite place for kiteboarding, swimming, and sunbathing.

4. The small island of Little Nevis, which sits off the coast of Nevis, is well-known for its isolated beaches. The beaches are a well-liked location for snorkeling, swimming, and sunbathing.

5. Dick's Bay is a beach on Nevis' north shore that is renowned for both its tranquil seas and its stunning views of the Nevis Peak. The beach is a well-liked location for picnicking, swimming, and tanning.

7.5 Catamaran to Nevis

Numerous catamarans provide excursions to Nevis. Usually, these cruises leave from St. Kitts and travel an hour to get to Nevis.

The Caribbean Sea's stunning beauty may be seen in exquisite detail from the catamarans. They also provide a range of amenities, including dining options, bars, and sun loungers.

On a catamaran to Nevis, you can perform a variety of things, such as:

-* Unwind on the deck: Catamarans feature roomy decks where you can unwind and take in the sunshine.

-* Go for a swim in the ocean: The catamarans usually make a few stops when you go for a swim in the ocean.

-* Go scuba diving or snorkeling: Catamarans can take you to some of the top diving and snorkeling locations in the region.

-* Visit Nevis: Once you are there, you can take your time exploring the island.

The following specific tour companies provide catamaran trips to Nevis:

1.Charters to the Leeward Islands
2. Catamaran cruises in the Caribbean
3. Sailing Charters in St. Kitts and Nevis

The following elements should be taken into account while selecting a catamaran excursion to Nevis:

1. The tour's price
2. The facilities provided

3. Departure and arrival times

4. The tour's duration

5. The standing of the business

A fantastic way to experience the best of the Caribbean Sea is on a catamaran to Nevis. They provide for an enjoyable and tranquil day on the water.

8. Transportation And The Costs

8.1 Obtaining a Ticket to St. Kitts and Nevis

It's an exciting aspect of your journey to reach St. Kitts and Nevis, two stunning Caribbean islands, and it sets the setting for an unforgettable holiday. These alluring locations are renowned for their stunning natural surroundings, fascinating histories, and welcoming cultures. Here is detailed information on how to go to St. Kitts and Nevis to assist you in making travel arrangements.

1. Arrival via Air:
- Robert L. The Robert L. Bradshaw International Airport on St. Kitts is where the majority of visitors from abroad land in St. Kitts and Nevis. The principal entry point to the islands is this cutting-edge airport, which accepts flights from several international locations,

including the United States, Canada, the United Kingdom, and other Caribbean states.

2. Flights out of important Hubs

- Direct flights to St. Kitts are available from several significant U.S. cities, including Miami, New York, Atlanta, and Charlotte. Regular services are provided by airlines like American Airlines, Delta, and United.

- From Canada: Air Canada frequently operates direct flights from Toronto to St. Kitts for Canadian passengers.

There are no direct flights from Europe to St. Kitts and Nevis, but you can connect through one of the continent's major cities, such as London or Paris. The two most popular airlines for these flights are British Airways and Air France.

3. Moving to Nevis:

- Travelers to Nevis can take a quick cab journey from St. Kitts to Basseterre, which is home to the island's ferry station. Between St. Kitts and Nevis, there are frequent boat services that run every 45 minutes or so. The picturesque boat journey is a quick way to go to Nevis and provides breathtaking views of both islands.

4. Private vessels and voyages:
- Private yachts and cruise ships can also reach St. Kitts and Nevis. The islands' marinas and ports are well-equipped to receive boaters and cruise visitors. Many Caribbean cruises stop at Basseterre, St. Kitts, which has a thriving cruise port.

5. Ferry: St. Kitts and Nevis can be reached by ferry as well. From Basseterre, St. Kitts, the ferry travels to Charlestown, Nevis.

Depending on the form of transportation you use, going to St. Kitts and Nevis will cost you a different amount. Typically, airfare is the most expensive method, while ferries are the least expensive.

8.2 Island-specific Transportation Options

There are several different ways to move around once you are in St. Kitts or Nevis.

1. The most popular method of transportation on both islands is by taxi. Taxis have meters, and the prices are reasonable.

2. Bus: On both islands, there are a few bus routes that run. Despite being less expensive than taxis, buses lack consistency.

3. Rent a car: If you want more flexibility, this is an option. On both islands, there are numerous automobile rental companies.

4. Bicycle: You can rent a bicycle if you're seeking a more environmentally friendly mode of transportation. Both islands have a large number of bike rental shops.

8.3 Transportation Costs and Budgeting

Depending on the form of transportation you select, the cost of travel within St. Kitts and Nevis will change. Here are some approximate prices:

* Taxi: $2 to $3 per mile
* Bus: $1–$2 for each ride
* Daily rates for a rental car range from $40 to $60.
* Rent a bike for about $10 to $15 per day.

The following things should be taken into account when creating a transportation budget:

-* The duration of your stay in St. Kitts & Nevis.
-* The destinations you want to see
-* Your preferred method of transportation
-* The price of getting around the islands by car.

Having cash on hand is also a smart idea because certain taxi and bus drivers might not accept credit cards.

Here are some suggestions for setting a transportation budget:

1.A resort may provide shuttle service to and from the airport and other well-known locations if you are staying there. This can help you avoid paying for cabs.

2. Renting a car is a smart idea if you want to do a lot of exploring. You'll be free to travel whenever and wherever you desire as a result. However, it's critical to understand how much insurance and a rental automobile will cost.

3. You might think about riding the bus if you're on a tight budget. Despite being less expensive than taxis, buses lack consistency.

4. You can split the cost of cabs and rental cars if you're traveling in a group. This can help you save money.

9. Accommodation And Prices

9.1 Available Types of Accommodation

St. Kitts and Nevis offers a wide range of lodging choices to fit every need and preference.

1. Resorts: Both islands have a variety of resorts, from opulent all-inclusive to reasonably priced alternatives. Swimming pools, dining establishments, and bars are common features of resorts.

2. Hotels: Both islands are home to numerous hotels that provide a range of features and services. For vacationers who prefer more flexibility than a resort offers, hotels are an excellent choice.

3. There are several bed and breakfasts on both islands, which provide a more individualized and private experience. For tourists who wish to get a taste of the local way of life, bed & breakfasts are a good choice.

4. Villas: Both islands provide a variety of villas that can be rented. For tourists who desire more room and privacy, villas are a good choice.

5. Additionally, both islands provide a good amount of Airbnb listings. For tourists who wish to cut costs while traveling, AirBnB is a smart choice.

9.2 Hotels & Resorts

The most common lodging options in St. Kitts and Nevis are resorts and hotels. They provide a wide range of amenities and services, making them a wonderful choice for tourists seeking a stress-free getaway.

In St. Kitts, a few of the more well-known resorts are as follows:

1. The Ritz-Carlton St. Kitts: Situated on a private peninsula with breathtaking views of the Caribbean Sea, this luxurious resort is one of the world's top destinations.

2. The St. Kitts Marriott Resort & Spa: Situated on a gorgeous beach, this resort provides a range of services and activities.

3. The Royal St. Kitts Hotel & Casino, is a resort with several dining options and a prime location in Basseterre.

In Nevis, a few of the most well-known hotels are:

1. The Four Seasons Nevis, a five-star hotel with breathtaking views of Nevis Peak and a private beach.

2. The Nisbet Plantation Beach Resort: Situated on a lovely beach, this resort provides a range of services and activities.

3. The Montpelier Plantation Inn, is a boutique hotel with a charming and tranquil ambiance in the center of Nevis.

9.3 Inns and Bed and Breakfasts

For tourists seeking a more private and individualized experience, guesthouses and bed and breakfasts (B&Bs) are a wonderful choice. They frequently provide a hearty breakfast and are situated in more residential areas, so you can get a feel for the community.

In St. Kitts, some of the most well-liked guesthouses and B&Bs are:

1. The Old House Inn, a bed & breakfast with exquisite rooms and a sumptuous breakfast, and situated in the center of Basseterre. The inn also boasts a pool and a wonderful garden.

2. The Montpelier Guesthouse: Situated in the center of Nevis, this inn provides breathtaking views of Nevis Peak.

3. The Golden Lemon Inn: This B&B is situated in a peaceful location of St. Kitts and provides cozy accommodations and a welcoming environment.

4. Conaree Village, St. Kitts, is home to The Fern Tree Bed & Breakfast. It is a serene inn with a magnificent view of the Caribbean Sea. The inn also features a sun deck and a pool.

5. The Seaview Inn is housed in a relaxed hotel that offers free WiFi and a quiet restaurant/bar. It is situated in St. Kitts' Basseterre.

9.4 Vacation Homes and Rentals

For tourists who desire more room and privacy, vacation rentals and villas are a good choice. They are a fantastic choice for families or groups of friends because they frequently have a kitchen, living room, and numerous bedrooms.

In St. Kitts, some of the most well-liked holiday homes and villas are as follows:

1. The Sugar Mill Estate, which has 4 bedrooms, 4 bathrooms, a swimming pool, and a tennis court, is

situated on a working sugar plantation and offers breathtaking views of the Caribbean Sea.

2. The Nisbet Plantation Beach Club: This property, which is situated on a lovely beach and offers a range of amenities like a swimming pool and a tennis court, features three bedrooms and three bathrooms.

3. The Montpelier Plantation Inn: Situated in the center of Nevis, this villa provides breathtaking views of Nevis Peak. There are 5 bedrooms and 5 bathrooms in the villa.

4. The Montpelier Beach Villa has spectacular views of Nevis Peak and is situated on a lovely beach. There are 4 bathrooms and 4 bedrooms in the villa.

5. In a quiet location in Nevis, The Ottley's Plantation Inn provides breathtaking views of the Caribbean Sea. There are 3 bathrooms and 3 bedrooms in the villa.

9.5 Options for Camping and Ecotourism

1. Nevis National Park: The endangered St. Kitts green monkey can be found in this park along with a variety of other plants and animals. In the park, there are numerous hiking trails and camping spots.

2. Sandy Point National Park is a park with a mangrove swamp and several beaches that are situated on the easternmost point of St. Kitts. In the park, there are numerous hiking trails and camping spots.

3. Brimstone Hill Fortress is a fort from the 17th century with breathtaking views of the Caribbean Sea, and it is a UNESCO World Heritage Site. In addition to camping spaces, the fort has several hiking paths.

4. The bougainvillea, which is St. Kitts' emblematic flower, is one of the many plants and flowers that call the St. Kitts Botanical Gardens home. In the gardens, there are numerous hiking trails and camping areas.

5. Nevis Plantation Inn: This inn provides environmentally friendly lodgings in addition to a range of activities like biking, hiking, and bird viewing.

9.6 Average Hotel Prices and Booking Advice

The type of lodging you select, the time of year you travel, and the amenities you need will all affect the average cost of lodging in St. Kitts and Nevis. However, a regular room at a hotel or resort can cost anything from $100 to $500 per night.

Additional information about St. Kitts and Nevis lodging pricing and suggestions for making reservations are provided below:

A. Average lodging expenses:
1. Standard rooms at resorts and hotels cost between $100 and $500 per night.

2. Guesthouses and B&Bs: Standard rooms cost between $50 and $150 a night.

3. The weekly cost of a standard villa in vacation rentals ranges from $1,000 to $5,000.

4. Camping: A campsite costs $20 to $40 per night.

B. Booking advice

1. Reserve your lodging in advance, especially from December to April, when demand is at its highest.

2. Take into account your budget and the kind of lodging you're seeking.

3. To get a sense of what to anticipate, read traveler evaluations.

4. Evaluate costs on various travel websites and agencies.

When making hotel reservations in St. Kitts and Nevis, keep the following additional considerations in mind:

1.* Depending on when you travel, the cost of lodging can change. The most expensive months are December through April, which is peak season. The off-season, when prices are lower, lasts from May to November.

2. * The price of lodging may also change based on the area. The cost of lodging in Basseterre, the capital of St. Kitts, is often more than it is elsewhere on the island.

3. * You may be able to save money on food and drink by staying at one of the all-inclusive resorts in St. Kitts and Nevis.

4. * Renting a car is a smart idea if you want to do a lot of exploring. You'll be free to travel whenever and wherever you desire as a result.

10. Outdoor Recreation

10.1 Beaches and Water Activities

Beautiful beaches that are great for swimming, tanning, and water sports can be found on St. Kitts and Nevis. In St. Kitts, a few of the more well-known beaches are as follows:

1. Beach Pinney
2. Coconut Beach
3. Bay Fonseca
4. Beach Nevis
5. Frank's Bay

In St. Kitts and Nevis, some of the most popular water activities include:

1. Snorkeling: Due to the clean seas and abundant marine life, St. Kitts and Nevis offers several chances for snorkeling.

2. Scuba diving: St. Kitts and Nevis offers a variety of dive locations for all levels of divers, from novice to expert.

3. Windsurfing: The trade winds of St. Kitts make for great conditions for this popular activity.

4. Kitesurfing: The trade winds of St. Kitts make for great conditions for this sport, which is also quite well-liked there.

5. Sailing a Hobie Cat is an excellent way to discover the waters around St. Kitts and Nevis.

10.2 Diving and Snorkeling Excursions

The diving and snorkeling in the Caribbean are some of the best on St. Kitts and Nevis. A superb underwater experience is provided by the clean waters and a variety of marine life.

The following are some of the top snorkeling locations in St. Kitts:

1. The Narrows is a confined passageway that connects St. Kitts and Nevis and is home to numerous coral reefs and fish.

2. Due to the quiet, beautiful waters at Pinney's Beach, snorkeling is very common there.

3. A variety of fish and coral reefs can be seen in the protected Coral Gardens area off the coast of St. Kitts.

In St. Kitts and Nevis, some of the top dive sites are:
1. The RMS Rhone:* Divers of all skill levels frequent this wreckage, which is situated off the coast of St. Kitts.

2. The Indian River is an interesting and difficult dive, and it is situated off the west coast of St. Kitts.

3. The Challenger Wreck is a well-known diving site for expert divers and is situated off the coast of Nevis.

10.3 Yachting & Sailing Experiences

Sailors and boat lovers frequently travel to St. Kitts and Nevis. Ideal sailing conditions are provided by the clean waters and consistent trade winds.

St. Kitts and Nevis offers a wide variety of sailing and yachting excursions, from day outings to multi-day leases. Among the most popular choices are:

1. From St. Kitts to Nevis, a popular day trip, you can go by boat. You may take in the sights of the islands and the nearby waterways as you travel.

2. The Caribbean can be sailed if you have more time. You can rent a boat and do this. This is a fantastic opportunity to see some of the top snorkeling and diving locations while exploring the islands.

3. Yachting Competitions: The annual St. Kitts & Nevis Regatta is just one of the yachting competitions that take

place on St. Kitts and Nevis. If you have any interest in sailing, you should watch this event.

10.4 Nature and Hiking Trails

There are a variety of basic to difficult hiking and natural routes on St. Kitts and Nevis. Among the most well-liked trails are:

1. The tallest mountain in St. Kitts and Nevis, Nevis Peak, provides breathtaking views of the islands. Although difficult, the ascent to the summit is worthwhile.

2. Brimstone Hill Fortress is a fort from the 17th century with breathtaking views of the Caribbean Sea, and it is a UNESCO World Heritage Site. The fort has several hiking trails.

3. Sandy Point National Park is a park with a mangrove swamp and several beaches that are situated on the

easternmost point of St. Kitts. In the park, there are many hiking trails.

4. The bougainvillea, which is St. Kitts' emblematic flower, is one of the many plants and flowers that call the St. Kitts Botanical Gardens home. In the gardens, there are many walking paths.

5. On the western side of St. Kitts, you can go along the picturesque Fig Tree Drive, which passes through a rainforest. You can choose a variety of hiking paths that are accessible from the road.

10.5 Tennis and Golf

Golfers and tennis players love to travel to St. Kitts and Nevis. Both islands have several top-notch tennis courts and golf courses.

Golfing

In St. Kitts, some of the top golf courses are as follows:

1. On St. Kitts' western coast, there is a championship golf course called Royal St. Kitts Golf Club.

2. On St. Kitts' eastern shore, there is a par-72 golf course called Frigate Bay Golf Club.

3. On Nevis' southern coast, there is a par-72 golf course called Nevis Plantation Golf Club.

Tennis

In St. Kitts, some of the top tennis courts are:

1. Tennis courts are available for use by visitors at the St. Kitts Marriott Resort & Spa.

2. Two tennis courts are available for use by visitors at The Old House Inn.

3. Two tennis courts are offered to visitors at the Nevis Plantation Inn.

10.6 Adventure and Zip-lining Parks

Many zip-lining and adventure parks may be found on St. Kitts and Nevis. Numerous sports, including zip line, rappelling, and hiking, are available in these parks.

Zip-lining

In St. Kitts, some of the top zip-lining parks are:

1. Nevis Extreme Adventures: This park has beginner- to advanced-level zip-lining courses.

2. St. Kitts Zipline Adventure: You may zip through the rainforest on this park's lone zip-lining course.

Parks with Adventure

In St. Kitts, some of the top adventure parks are:

1. Ziplining, rappelling, and trekking are just a few of the thrilling activities available at Nevis.

2. Hiking, motorcycling, and bird viewing are just a few of the activities available at St. Kitts Eco Adventures.

Numerous tour companies provide excursions to St. Kitts and Nevis if you're interested in activities like zip-lining, adventure parks, golf, tennis, or any of the other sports mentioned. These outings often come with all the necessary gear and training.

11. Events and Festivals

11.1 Carnival Celebrations Held Annually

The yearly carnival celebrations in St. Kitts and Nevis are well-known for being a vivid and colorful celebration of Caribbean culture. The celebrations normally occur between December and January and include a range of activities, such as:

- Carnival parades: The parade, which includes vibrant floats, costumes, and music, is the festival's centerpiece. Competitions for the best costumes are held in several categories, including traditional, masquerade, and kid's costumes.

On all of the islands, there are street celebrations where people dance, drink, and have fun.

All of the gatherings feature live music and dancing, and attendees of all ages take part in the celebrations.

All of the events offer a variety of food and beverages, including foods and beverages that are typically associated with the Caribbean.

The Sugar Mas

The most well-known carnival event in St. Kitts is called Sugar Mas, and it lasts for two weeks in late December and early January. The festival, which honors the island's sugar cane economy, includes several activities, such as:

- The J'Ouvert Jam is Sugar Mas' kickoff celebration, and it consists of a street party featuring music, dancing, and costumes.

- The King and Queen Competition: The King and Queen of Sugar Mas are chosen in this competition, which also includes calypso, soca, and limbo performances.

- The Sugar Mas Grand Parade, the festival's centerpiece, is a vibrant parade of floats, costumes, and music.
- The After-Party is an event that happens following the Grand Parade and includes live music and dancing.

Anyone traveling to St. Kitts during the Christmas season must attend the lively and spectacular event known as Sugar Mas.

11.2 Festivals of Music and Culture

St. Kitts and Nevis also organizes a variety of other music and cultural festivals throughout the year in addition to carnival. These celebrations of the island's rich culture and legacy include a variety of activities, such as:

1. Jazz Festival: This event, which takes place in February, presents a range of jazz performances by both domestic and foreign performers.

2. World Music Festival: This event, which is held in March, showcases a range of world music performances by musicians from all around the world.

3. Calypso and Soca Festival: Held in April, this event showcases a range of calypso and soca performances by St. Kitts and Nevis-based musicians.

4. Nevis Heritage Festival: This event, which takes place in July, honors Nevis's history and culture.

5. The St. Kitts Music Festival is a December event that offers musical performances by both local and foreign performers.

11.3 Celebrations of Local Festivals

Throughout the year, St. Kitts and Nevis also celebrates several regional festivals in addition to the celebrations of the public holidays and carnival. These celebrations of the island's rich culture and legacy include a variety of activities, such as:

1. Kittitian Independence Day is observed on September 19 and honors St. Kitts and Nevis' 1983 declaration of independence from the United Kingdom.

2. Nevis Cultural Fair: This festival honors the history and culture of Nevis and is held in July.

3. Black San' Bang-A-Lang: This festival honors the liberation of slaves in the Caribbean and is held in April.

4. Green Valley Festival: This event, which takes place in May, honors the history and culture of St. Kitts' Green Valley neighborhood.

5. Flowers and plants from St. Kitts and Nevis are displayed in this event, which is held in November.

11.4 National and Religious Holidays

In St. Kitts and Nevis, the following days are observed as national and religious holidays:

1. New Year's Day: This holiday, which is observed on January 1st, ushers in a new year.

2. Good Friday is a holiday that honors the crucifixion of Jesus Christ and is observed the Friday before Easter Sunday.

3. Easter Sunday is a feast that honors the resurrection of Jesus Christ and is observed the Sunday following Good Friday.

4. Easter Monday is a day of celebration that falls on the Monday after Easter Sunday.

5. Labor Day: This holiday, which honors the contributions of labor, is observed on the first Monday in May.

6. Whit Monday is a day of celebration that falls on the 50th day following Easter Sunday.

7. Corpus Christi: This feast honors the Eucharist and is observed on the Thursday after Trinity Sunday.

8. Independence Day: This holiday, which is observed on September 19th, honors the year 1983 when St. Kitts and Nevis gained their independence from the United Kingdom.

9. Christmas Day: This holiday, which honors the birth of Jesus Christ, is observed on December 25.

10. Boxing Day: A day of giving to those in need, this holiday is observed on December 26.

Check the dates of these holidays if you are planning a trip to the islands so that you can schedule your activities appropriately.

12. Perfect 7 Days Itinerary

Day 1: Getting to Know Basseterre, the Capital

Begin your journey at St. Kitts' lovely capital, Basseterre. Start by going to Independence Square, the city's center, which is encircled by old structures in the Georgian style. Learn about the history and culture of the island by exploring the National Museum, which is housed in a former sugar mill.

Take a stroll through the busy streets to locate local markets, stores, and cafes. St. George's Anglican Church is a beautiful site of worship with a rich past that you shouldn't miss.

Enjoy lunch with Caribbean cuisine at a nearby restaurant. Go to Brimstone Hill Fortress National Park in the afternoon, which is a UNESCO World Heritage Site. This fortress is in excellent condition, and it provides stunning views and information about the island's colonial past.

Day 2: Beach Exploration and Water Sports

Go beach hopping and engage in water sports on your second day. Start in the lovely Frigate Bay, where you may go swimming or snorkeling or simply unwind on the golden sands. Discover the busy beach bars and beachside restaurants at the neighboring South Frigate Bay.

Go to Cockleshell Bay in the afternoon for a peaceful beach experience or board a boat to Nevis. Explore vibrant coral reefs while snorkeling and enjoying a Caribbean-style beach BBQ.

Day 3: Historical Sites and landmarks

Discover the historical sites and landmarks of St. Kitts. Start at Romney Manor, a gorgeously renovated plantation home encircled by verdant grounds. The magnificent Samaná Fortress should not be missed, nor should the adjoining Wingfield Estate, where you can still see the remains of a former sugar plantation.

Continue to St. Thomas Anglican Church, which is distinguished by its unusual exterior of black lava stone. Visit Bloody Point, a location with historical significance connected to the Carib Indian Wars, while taking a picturesque drive.

Visit the picturesque village of Old Road to cap off the day, where you can learn about regional culture and artwork at the Caribelle Batik studio.

Day 4: Exploring the Natural World

Discover St. Kitts' breathtaking natural beauty. The island's highest peak, Mount Liamuiga, is to be reached first via a climb. The walk leads through luxuriant woods, and the peak rewards you with breathtaking panoramas.

Visit the Black Rocks, an eye-catching volcanic rock formation along the shore, after lunch. Enjoy the sea breeze while exploring the distinctive geological characteristics.

Visit the Botanical Gardens' Rainforest Conservatory in the afternoon to get a close-up look at tropical plants and animals.

Day 5: Nevis Island Excursion

Visit the nearby island of Nevis for the day. Enjoy the ferry ride between the two islands, which is scenic. Discover Charlestown, the capital of Nevis, and its historic landmarks, such as St. Paul's Anglican Church and the Alexander Hamilton House.

The scenic Pinney's Beach, known for its golden beaches and beachside bars, is a great place to unwind. At one of the charming restaurants, savor the regional Nevisian food.

Day 6: Adventures and Outdoor Activities

On St. Kitts, embrace outdoor adventures. Start by ziplining through a rainforest's canopy or riding a horse along a beautiful track. Off-road ATV rides are good for thrill-seekers.

Visit the Royal St. Kitts Golf Club in the afternoon for a round of golf with breathtaking views of the Caribbean. Finish the day with a catamaran cruise at sunset that includes refreshments and snorkeling.

Day 7: Spa Retreats and Relaxation

Enjoy a day of wellness and leisure. Book a spa day at one of the opulent resorts to take advantage of the relaxing atmosphere and restorative services. Take a relaxing nap by the water or on the sand while drinking tropical drinks.

Enjoy a sumptuous seafood feast and live Caribbean music at a beachside restaurant to cap off your trip. Before you go, think back on your fantastic week in St. Kitts & Nevis and relish the memories.

13. Conclusion

In conclusion, St. Kitts and Nevis are great locations for tourists looking for a Caribbean vacation because they provide a mesmerizing fusion of natural beauty, ancient history, and genuine friendliness. These islands offer something for everyone, from the charming town of Basseterre to the beautiful beaches and verdant rainforests.

You may experience the local culture, eat delectable cuisine, and partake in exhilarating outdoor adventures while exploring St. Kitts and Nevis. The islands offer a wide variety of adventures, from diving in beautiful waters to hiking to the top of Mount Liamuiga to just lounging on the golden dunes.

A responsible and pleasurable trip requires consideration for the environment, observance of regional customs and etiquette, and knowledge of health and safety concerns. Additionally, you can improve your entire experience by carefully planning your trip, taking travel insurance into account, and heeding general travel advice.

Remember to relish the moment, embrace the warmth of the Caribbean spirit, and make lifelong memories in this tropical paradise as you travel to St. Kitts and Nevis. These islands offer a slice of paradise that will leave you with treasured memories for years to come, whether you're looking for adventure, relaxation, or a cultural excursion. Travel safely.

Made in United States
Troutdale, OR
11/28/2023

15081031R00090